COLD CALLS

COLD CALLS

War Music continued

CHRISTOPHER LOGUE

faber and faber

First published in 2005
by Faber and Faber Limited
3 Queen Square London WC1N 3AU
Published in the United States by Faber and Faber Inc.,
an affiliate of Farrar, Straus and Giroux LLC, New York

Photoset by RefineCatch Ltd, Bungay, Suffolk
Printed in England by T. J. International Ltd, Padstow, Cornwall

Audiologue, a seven-CD set of recordings by Christopher Logue
that includes the full text of *War Music*, is available from
Unknown Public Limited, Suite 8, Grove House, London W10H 5BZ

A CIP record for this book
is available from the British Library

ISBN 0-571-20277-2

2 4 6 8 10 9 7 5 3

ACKNOWLEDGEMENTS

Craig Raine edited the text, Charles Boyle, James Campbell and Paul Keegan commented on it, and Mildred Marney processed it; Ferdinand Mount, Dr Michael Rogers and the late Sir Stephen Tumin supported grant applications on my behalf, and the work was sustained throughout by Mark Getty and Transon Ltd.

Parts of the text have appeared in the *Times Literary Supplement* and *Poetry* (Chicago).

CL

COLD CALLS

Many believe in the stars.

Take Quinamid
The son of a Dardanian astrologer
Who disregarded what his father said
And came to Troy in a taxi.

Gone

Odysseus to Greece:

'Hector has never fought this far from Troy.
We want him further out. Beyond King Ilus' tower.
So walk him to the centre of the plain and, having killed him,
Massacre the Trojans there.'

'Ave!'

Immediately beyond the ridge is Primrose Hill
Where Paris favoured Aphrodite.

'Take it,' said Hector.

Greece shouted: 'Hurry up!'
Troy shouted: 'Wait for us!'

See,
Far off,
Masts behind the half-built palisade.
   Then
Nearer yourselves
Scamánder's ford
From which the land ascends
Then merges with the centre of the plain –
The tower (a ruin) its highest point.

Heaven.
Bad music.
Queen Hera is examining her gums.
Looking in through a window
Teenaged Athena, God's favourite child, says:
   'Trouble for Greece.'

   They leave.

Sea.
Sky.
The sunlit snow.

   Two armies on the plain.
Hector, driven by Lutie,
His godchild and his nephew,
Going from lord to Trojan lord:

   'The ships by dark.'

4

The ruined tower.

In front of it –
Their banners rising one by one.
One after one, and then another one –
50,000 Greeks.

And on a rise in front of Greece
Two of its hero lords:

Ajax the Great of Salamis
Behind his shield –
   As 50 Trojan shields
Topped with blue plumes, swivelling their points,
Come up the rise –
   Lord Teucer (5 feet high and 5 feet wide)
Loading his bow,
Peering round Ajax' shield,
Dropping this Trojan plume or that,
Ordering his archers to lie flat,
Promising God as many sheep as there are sheep to count
If he can put a shaft through Hector's neck.

   Prosperity!
Beneath the blue, between the sea, the snow, there Hector is
Surrendering the urn of one he has just killed
To one who thought that he had killed the same.

   Lord Teucer's eye/Prince Hector's throat.
But God would not. The bowstring snaps.

Outside God's inner court.
The lake-eyed Queen, the Daughter, still in line.

The first so angry she can hardly speak.
A voice:
'The Wife, the Daughter.'
'You go. His face will make me heave.'

God's court.
Her blood-red mouth, her ice-white face:

'Serene and Dignified Grandee.'
'Papa to you.'

'Papa' – His hand –
'I know you do not want the Holy Family visiting the plain.
But some of us would like to help the Greeks.
They lost their champion she.
Thousands of them have died. Now they are in retreat. Please
    look.'

The plain.

'You will come back the moment that I call?'
'Of course, Papa.'
'Then . . . yes. Encourage Greece.
But voices only.
Words. Shouts. That sort of thing. A move – and home you
    come.'
'Of course, Papa.'

The plain.

Lord Teucer's archers hidden in its grass.

Chylábborak, Lord Hector's brother-in-law, to his blue plumes:

6

'Move!'
'Move!'
And on their flanks, between the sea and snow,
Led by Teléspiax' silver yard
All Ilium's masks.

"Down came their points. Out came their battle cry.
And our cool Mr 5 × 5 called: 'Up.' And up we got
And sent our arrows into them,
That made them pirouette,
Topple back down the rise, leaving their dead
For some of us to strip, and some, the most,
To pause, to point, to plant, a third, a fourth
Volley into their naked backs. Pure joy!"

Chylábborak,
Holding his ground:
'Centre on me.
More die in broken than in standing ranks.
Apollo! Aphrodite! Our gods are out!
You taste the air, you taste their breath!
The Greek fleet, ours, by dark!'

Then he is ringed.

See an imperial pig harassed by dogs.
How, like a masterchef his crêpes,
He tosses them; then as they paddle back
Eviscerates, and flips them back again.
Likewise Chylábborak the Greeks who rushed.

Hector has seen it. As –
Beneath the blue, the miles of empty air,

7

Him just one glitter in that glittering mass –
The hosts begin to merge.

Fine dust clouds mixed with beams of light.
The Prince, down from his plate.
Either sides' arrows winging by:
    'Cover my back.'
Finding a gap,
Dismissing blows as gales do slates,
Then at a run, leaping into the ring,
Taking Chylábborak's hand:
    'If you don't mind?'

Agamemnon:
    'Our time has come. God keeps his word.
Fight now as you have never fought.
We will be at Troy's gates by dusk,
Through them by dark,
By dawn, across our oars,
As we begin our journey home,
Watching the windmills on its Wall
Turn their sails in flames.'

Heaven. The Wife. The Daughter.

    Hands release black lacquer clasps inlaid with particles of
        gold.
    Silk sheaths – with crashing waves and fishscales woven on a
        navy ground –

Flow on the pavement.

Hands take their hands

While other hands supply

Warwear,

Their car,

And put the reins into Athena's hands.

'. . . Troy's gates by dusk,
Through them by dark . . .'

The Hours, the undeniable,
Open the gates of Paradise.

Beyond

The wastes of space.

Before

The blue.

Below

Now near

The sea, the snow.

All time experts in hand-to-hand action –
Fricourt, Okinawa, Stalingrad West –
Could not believe the battle would gain.
But it did.

   Chylábborak's ring is ringed. And then no ring at all.
Some Trojans raise their hands in prayer;
Some Panachéans shout for joy and wait to drag the corpses
      off.
   Lutie, alone, the reins in one, his other hand
Hacking away the hands that grab his chariot's bodywork,
Rearing his horses, Starlight and Bertie, through,
      To,
      Yes,
   Chylábborak up; rescued;
Prince Hector covering. Then:

   'Zoo-born wolf! Front for a family of thieves!'
Lord Diomed, on foot, with Sethynos, his next.
   My Lutie answering:
   'Be proud, Prince Hector is your Fate.'
(Which will be so, though Lutie will not see it.)
   Chylábborak and Hector do not want to disappoint this oily
      pair:
   'Here come the Sisters Karamazov, Spark.'
Chylábborak said, 'Let's send them home in halves.'
And jumped back down.

   Around the tower 1000 Greeks, 1000 Ilians; amid their
      swirl,
His green hair dressed in braids, each braid
Tipped with a little silver bell, note

Nyro of Simi – the handsomest of all the Greeks, save A.
   The trouble was, he had no fight. He dashed from fight to
      fight,
Struck a quick blow, then dashed straight out again.
Save that this time he caught,
As Prince Aenéas caught his breath,
That Prince's eye; who blocked his dash,
And as lord Panda waved and walked away,
Took his head off his spine with a backhand slice –
Beautiful stuff . . . straight from the blade . . .
   Still, as it was a special head,
Mowgag, Aenéas' minder –
Bright as a box of rocks, but musical –
Spiked it, then hoisted it, and twizzling the pole
Beneath the blue, the miles of empty air,
Marched to the chingaling of its tinklers,
A majorette, towards the Greeks, the tower.

A roar of wind across the battlefield.

A pause.

And then

   Scattering light,
The plain turned crystal where their glidepath stopped,
Queen Hera shrills: 'Typhoid for Troy!'
And through poor Nyro's wobbling mouth
Athena yells:

   'Slew of assidious mediocrities!
Meek Greeks!
Hector will burn your ships to warm his soup!'

It is enough.

Centre-plain wide,
Lit everywhere by rays of glorious light,
They rushed their standards into Ilium,
Diomed (for once) swept forward;
Converting shame to exaltation with his cry:

'Never – to Helen's gold without her self!
Never – to Helen's self without her gold!'

Mowgag well slain.
Hewn through his teeth, his jaw slashed off,
And Nyro's head beside him in the grass.

When Nyro's mother heard of this
She shaved her head; she tore her frock; she went outside
Ripping her fingernails through her cheeks:
Then down her neck; her chest; her breasts;
And bleeding to her waist ran round the shops,
Sobbing:
'God, kill Troy.
Console me with its death.
Revenge is all I have.
My boy was kind. He had his life to live.
I will not have the chance to dance in Hector's blood,
But let me hear some have before I die.'

'I saw her running round.
I took the photograph.
It summed the situation up.
He was her son.
They put it out in colour. Right?
My picture went around the world.'

Down the shaft of the shot in his short-staved bow
Lord Panda has been follow-spotting Diomed.

Between 'her self'/'her gold' he shoots.
It hits. And as its barbs protrude through Dio's back
Aenéas hears lord Panda shout:
    'He bleeds! The totem Greek! Right-shoulder-front!
How wise of Artemis to make
Panda her matador! Her numero uno! Moi!'

    Diomed hit,
The heart went out of those who followed him
And they fell back.

Shields all round

Diomed on his knees

Lifting his hands:

'Sister and wife of God'

As Sethynos breaks off the arrow-head

'Eliminate my pain.'

Settles his knee beneath his hero's shoulderblades

'Let me kill that oaf who claims my death'

Bridges his nape with one hand

'Before it comes with honour to my name.'

13

Then with his other hand
In one long strong slow pull
Drew the shank back, and out.

She heard his prayer.

Before their breathless eyes
His blood ran back into the pout the shank had left,
And to complete her miracle
Lord Diomed rose up between them, stood in the air,
Then hovered down onto his toes
Brimming with homicidal joy,
Imparting it to Greece.

Then Troy was driven back,
Trampling the half-stripped still-masked carcasses
Hatching the centre of the plain.

Aenéas/Panda.

'Get him.'

'*Get* him! I *got* him. *He is dead*. But there *he is*.'

And Diomed has spotted *them*.

'Calm down,' Aenéas said. 'Perhaps he is possessed.'

'What god would visit him?'

'So pray to yours – and try another shot.'

'*Huntress*,' lord Panda prays,
Bright-ankled god of nets and lines,
Of tangled mountains and of dark cascades . . . '

But Artemis was bored with him
And let him rise, still praying hard,
Into the downflight of the javelin
Diomed aired at Prince Aenéas.

Sunlit, it went through Panda's lips, out through his neck,
    and then –
As he was swivelling into a run – through Biblock's neck.
And so they fell; the lord, face up; the friend, face down,
Gripping the blood-smeared barb between his teeth,
Between the sea and snow.

'It will be ours by dusk!'

Aenéas covers them.

Eyeing his plate
– Technology you can enjoy –
Diomed found, and threw, a stone
As heavy as a cabbage made of lead,
That hit, and split, Aenéas' hip.
Who went down on one knee
And put his shield hand on the grass
And with his other hand covered his eyes.
Dido might have become a grandmother
And Rome not had its day, except,
As Diomed came on to lop his top
Aenéas' mama, Aphrodité (dressed
In grey silk lounge pyjamas piped with gold
And snakeskin flip-flops) stepped
Between him and the Greek.

A glow came from her throat, and from her hair
A fragrance that betokened the divine.
Stooping, she kissed him better, as
Queen Hera whispered: 'Greek, cut that bitch.'
And, Diomed, you did; nicking Love's wrist.

Studying the ichor as
It seeped across her pulse into her palm
Our Lady of the Thong lifted her other hand,
Removed a baby cobra from her hair
And dropped it, Diomed, onto your neck,
And saw its bite release its bane into your blood.
    Then nobody could say
Who Diomed fought for, or for what he fought.

    Rapt through the mass
Now shouting at the sky, now stomping on the plain,
He killed and killed and killed, Greek, Trojan, Greek.
Lord/less, shame/fame, both gone; and gone
Loyalty nurtured in the face of death,
The duty of revenge, the right to kill,
To jeer, to strip, to gloat, to be the first
To rally but the last to run, all gone –
And gone, our Lady Aphrodité, giggling.

    While everywhere, my Diomed,

You beat your fellow Greeks
Back down the long incline that leads to the Scamánder's
    ford,
Surely as when
Lit from the dark part of the sky by sudden beams,

A bitter wind
Detonates line by line of waves against the shore.

   No mind. Even as Teucer backed away
He kept his eyes on you, hearing you roar:
   'You feel the stress? You feel the fear?
Behold your enemy Greece! the Prince God loves!'
   See Teucer's bow. Hear Teucer's: 'This time lucky.' His –
But this time it was not our Father, God,
Who saved your life, my Prince.
   As Agamemnon cried:
   'The ships are safe.
Stand at the riverside's far bank.'
Teléspiax heard the rustle of lord Teucer's shot
And stood between yourself and it.

   His head was opened, egglike, at the back,
Mucked with thick blood, blood trickling from his mouth.
His last words were:
   'My Prince, your trumpeter has lost his breath.'

   'Our worst fear was his face would fade,' Teléspiax's father
      said.
'But it did not. We will remember it until we die.'

   'Give his instrument to Hogem,' Hector said, and went –
Lutie on reins – between the sea and snow,
Throwing his chariots wide, Scamánderwards,
As easily as others might a cloak.

   Diomed in this traffic, on his own,
Among his dead,
Their pools of blood, their cut-off body-parts,

Their cut-off heads,
Ashamed as his head cleared
To see Odysseus, Idomeneo, the Ajax – Big and Small –
Whipping away downslope, you shouting at Odysseus:
   'Where are you going with your back to the battle?'
Who shouted back, although he did not turn:
   'Look left!'
And there was Lutie driving Hector onto him.

   Certainly they would trample him, for certainly
Queen Hera's human, Diomed,
Would stand and die, except:
   'Arms up, young king –' Nestor, full tilt,
Reins round his tummy, leaning out '– and
Jump . . .' wrists locked '. . . You young are just . . .'
Swinging him up onto the plate '. . . too much.'

   'With your permission, Da?'
Nod. Drew. Then threw the chariot's javelin
As Lutie spun his wheels, and Hector threw –
Those skewers trading brilliance as they passed –
And missed – both vehicles slither-straightening,
Regaining speed, close, close, then driven apart
By empty cars careering off the incline,
Or stationary cars, their horses cropping grass.

   'Daddy, go slow. Hector will say I ran.'
   'But not the widows you have made.'

   And slow
   And low
Cruising the blue above this mix
Heaven's Queen and Ringsight-eyed Athene
Trumpeting down huge clouds of sound
As Hector's car rereached king Nestor's, and:

18

'What kept you, Prince?' Diomed offered as they came
        abreast:
'You went for a refreshing towel?'
And threw his axe, that toppled through the air, and, oh,
Hector, my Hector, as you thought:
'If Heaven helps me Heaven shows it loves the best,'
Parted your Lutie's mesh and smashed into his heart.

    What did you say as God called you to death,
Dear Lutie?

    'My Prince, I leave you driverless.'

    And put the reins into Hector's hands, and fled
Into oblivion

    As Hector with his other hand
Held what his Lutie was, upright, face forwards, in between
The chariot's rail and himself,
Shouting as he drove after them:

    'Loathsome Greek,
Your loathsome hair, your loathsome blood,
Your loathsome breath, your loathsome heart,
Jump in your loathsome ships,
I will come after you,
Come over the Aegean after you,
And find you though you hide inside
Your loathsome father's grave
And with my bare hands twist your loathsome head
Off your loathsome neck.'

    There was a Greek called Themion.
Mad about armour. If not armour, cars.
Of course he went to Troy. And Troy

Saw a stray spear transfix him as he drove.
  Companionably, his horses galloped up
On Starlight's side, and muddled Starlight down,
And Bertie down, and brought the Prince
(Still holding Lutie) down, as all the world
Hurried, as if by windheads, on towards Scamánder's ford.

Whether you reach it from the palisade
Or through the trees that dot the incline's last stretch
You hear Scamánder's voice before you see
What one may talk across on quiet days,
Its rippling sunspangled breadth
Streaming across the bars of pebbly sand
That form its ford
– Though on the Fleet's side deeper, darkly bright.

   And here
Tiptoeing from this bar to that,
Settling the cloudy sunshine of her hair,
Her towel retained by nothing save herself,
The God of Tops and Thongs
Our Lady Aphrodité came,
Her eyes brimful with tears.

Scamánder is astonished by his luck.

   'Beauty of Beauties, why are you weeping?'
   'I have been hurt, Scamánder.'
   'No . . .'
   'Humiliated.'
   'No.'
   'Me. A god. Just like yourself. Touched . . .'
   'Touched!'
   'By a man.'
   'A *man*!'
   'A Greek.'

'Death to all Greeks!'
'He cut me!'
'Sacrilege!
. . . But where?'
'I need your healing touch.'
'How can I help you if you do not show me where?'
'Moisten its lips and my wound will be healed.'
'You must say where!'
'Well . . .'
The towel has slipped an inch.
'I am afraid you will be disappointed.'
'Never.'
'Are you sure?'
'Yes!'
'You will not criticise me?'
'*No!*'
Her wrist upturned.
Out-turned.
Her opened palm.
Fanning the fingers of her other hand,
Stroking his spangles with her fingertips.
   'Goddess, I love you.
I have always loved you.
Say that you love me. Even a little.
I beg you. God grant it.'
   'I need your help, Scamánder.'
   'Take pity on me. Come into me.'
   'You have your nymphs.'
   'Bores! Bores!'
   'I might be nibbled by an eel!'
   'Death to all eels!'
The towel is down.
   'Step into me . . .
I love your toes . . . please let me kiss your toes . . .
Your little dinkum-inkum toes . . .'

'No one has kissed them so nicely, Scamánder.'
'And now your knees . . .'
'You tickle me . . .'
'And now your thighs!'
'Oh, oh, go on . . .'
'And now your bum!
Your Holy Bum! Your Sacred Bum!
The Bum of Paradise!'
'Oh, my Scamánder, I must have your help . . .'
'Anything!'
The towel goes curling off,
And as she floated on his stream
Our Lady Aphrodité said:
'At any moment now the Greeks will reach your Troy-side
    bank . . .'

Recall those sequences
When horsemen ride out of the trees and down into a stream
Somewhere in Kansas or Missouri, say.
So – save they were thousands, mostly on foot – the Greeks
Into Scamánder's ford.

Coming downstream,
A smallish wave

That passes

But

Scamánder's flow does not relapse.

Indeed

Almost without a sound
Its murmuring radiance became
A dark, torrential surge
Clouded with boulders, crammed with trees, as clamorous as
    if it were a sea,
That lifted Greece, then pulled Greece down,
Cars gone, masks gone, gone under, reappearing, gone:

'Onto your knees! Praise Hector for this flood!
The Prince God loves!' Prince Hector claims
As he comes through the trees.

They do.
Then up and run, thousands of them,
To hold those Greeks
Under until their bubbles stopped; while those swept off
Turned somersaults amid Scamánder's undertow.

The flat –

1000 yards of it between the river and the palisade.

The King:

'The Lord has not abandoned us.
To cross will be as bad for them.'

But it was not to be as bad for them.

Indeed,
As Hector drove towards Scamánder's brink,

And as – their banners rising one by one,
One after one and then another one –
He and all Ilium began to enter it,
The river reassumed its softly-spoken, smooth, sunspangled
  way.

  And Agamemnon cried:

  'God, what are You for?
What use are You to me?'

  As Hector cries:

  'Two miracles!
Your Prince is close to God!'

  And Hera to Athene:

  'Fog?'

  And fog came down.

  And most of Greece got out.

  Troy holding hands midstream.
An army peering through its masks.

  Miss Tops and Thongs to God:

  'Your Hera has . . .'

  And with a wish He turned the fog to light,

And with a word He called them back to Heaven.

Sky.
Snow.
The 1000 yards.
The palisade.

Hector:
  'I am your Prince.
My name means He-Who-Holds.
Troy. And the plain. And now the ships.
  For Troy!'
His battle cry
Rising into a common cry, that cry
Into a clamour, and that clamour to
Bayings of hatred.

  800 yards.

  The Child:
  'We are the Greeks. We fight to win. If one is lost,
Close his eyes, step over him, and kill his enemy.'

  800 yards.

  The Greeks are tiring.
Nestor is on his knees:

  'God of all Gods, Most Holy and Most High,
  If Greece has ever sacrificed fresh blood to you,
  Protect our ships.'

Soft music. Summertime. Queen Hera and Athene? Yes . . .

Some lesser gods
Observing their approach, approach,
Salaam, and then
Lead them –
Now both in black wraparound tops –
To God:

'Darling Daddy, here we are.'
'And' (Hera) 'here we stay
Until you stop that worthless Hector killing Greeks.'
Up steps Love.
Hera: 'Why is she wearing a tent?'
Love: 'Father, see this.' (Her wrist.)
'Human strikes god! Communism! The end of everything!'

'Darlings,' He said,
'You know that being a god means being blamed.
Do this – no good. Do that – the same. The answer is:
Avoid humanity.
Remember – I am God.
I see the bigger picture.'

'And I am Hera, Heaven's Queen,
Greece worships me.'

'Stuff Greece,' Love said.
'Your blubber-bummed wife with her gobstopper nipples
Cannot stand Troy because Troy's Paris put her last
When we stripped off for him.
As for the Ithacan boat-boy's undercurved preceptatrix,
She hates Troy because *my* statue stands on its acropolis.'

Hera: 'The cities' whores were taxed to pay for it.'
Love (Dropping onto her knees before Himself):
'Please . . . stop them harming Troy. The greatest city in the
   world.'

While Hera and Athene sang:

'Cleavage! Cleavage!
Queen of the Foaming Hole.
Mammoth or man or midge
She sucks from pole to pole.'

And God has had enough of it.

Lifting His scales He said:

'Hector will have his day of victory.'
Then crashed them to the ground.

7oo yards.

The palisade.

Its gate.

Late sunlight on gilt beaks.

'There's no escape from Troy.'
'Or from the plain at Troy.'

Begging for ransom, Trojan Hoti,
His arms around King Menelaos' knees.

King Agamemnon: 'Off.'

Then he punched Hoti in the face.
Then punched him in the face again.
And then again. And when he fell
King Agamemnon kicked him in the groin.
Kicking him in the groin with so much force
It took a step to follow up each kick.
Then pulled him up,
Then dragged him by his hair
This way and that,
Then left him, calling:
    'Finish him off.'
And someone did.

'I was 16. I said: "Where is Achilles?"
Hard as it is to share another's troubles when your own are
    pressing
Great Ajax took my hands in his and said:
"He loves us. He is with us. He will come." '

But he did not.

    Then Ajax to himself:
    'Dear Lord, you made me straight.
Give me the strength to last till dark.'

    The Prince: 'I get by everything I see.
Their war is lost.'

    It was.

Aenéas, Ábassee, Sarpédon, Gray,
Calling to one another down the line.
    Then, with a mighty wall of sound,

29

As if a slope of stones
Rolled down into a lake of broken glass
We Trojans ran at them.

 And now the light of evening has begun
To shawl across the plain:
Blue gray, gold gray, blue gold,
Translucent nothingnesses
Readying our space,
Within the deep, unchanging sea of space,
For Hesper's entrance, and the silver wrap.

   Covered with blood, mostly their own,
Loyal to death, reckoning to die
Odysseus, Ajax, Diomed,
Idomeneo, Nestor, Menelaos
And the King:

   'Do not die because others have died.'
   'Do not show them the palms of your hands.'

      'Achil!'
      'Achil!'
      'If he won't help us, Heaven help us.'

      'Stand still and *fight*.'
      'Feel shame in one another's eyes.'
      'I curse you, God. You are a liar, God.
   Troy will be yours by dark – immortal lies.'
      'Home!'
      'Home!'
      'There's no such place.'
      'You can't launch burning ships.'

'More men survive if no one runs.'

But that is what Greece did.

Dropping their wounded,
Throwing down their dead,
Their shields, their spears, their swords,
They ran.

Leaving their heroes tattered, filthy, torn

And ran

And ran

Above their cries:

'I am the Prince! The victory is mine!'

Chylábborak:

'Do not take cowardice for granted.'

Scarce had he said it, when
His son, Kykéon, standing next to him
Took Ajax' final spear cast in his chest.

'I shall not wear your armour, Sir,' he said.
And died.

'My son is dead.'

The Prince:

'Hector is loved by God.'

And Greece, a wall of walking swords,
But walking backwards,
Leaving the plain in silence
And in tears.

Idomeneo,
Running back out at those Trojans who came too close:

'You know my name. Come look for me. And boy,
The day you do will be the day you die.'

Hector to Troy:
'Soldiers! –
Unmatched my force, unconquerable my will.
After ten years of days, in one long day
To be remembered for as many days
As there are days to come, this is my day,
Your Hector's day. Troy given back to Troy.
My day of victory!'
    And when the cheering died:
    'Some say: destroy Greece now. But I say no.
Out of your cars. Eat by your fires.
Two hundred fires! Around each fire
Five hundred men!
    'The sound of grindstones turning through the night,
The firelight that stands between our blades,
So let King Agamemnon's own hold hands
And look into each other's frightened eyes.
    'True God! Great Master of the Widespread Sky!
If only You would turn
Me into a god,

As You, through me,
Tomorrow by their ships
Will see Greece die.'

Silence.

A ring of lights.

Within

Immaculate

In boat-cloaks lined with red

King Agamemnon's lords –

The depression of retreat,
The depression of returning to camp.

   Him at the centre of their circle
Sobbing,
Shouting:

   'We must run for it!'

   Dark glasses in parked cars.

'King Agamemnon of Mycenae,
God called, God raised, God recognised,
You are a piece of shit,' Diomed said.

   Silence again.

35

'Let us praise God,' lord Ajax said,
'That Hector stopped before he reached the ships.'

Silence again.

Then

Nestor
(Putting his knee back in):

'Paramount Agamemnon, King of kings,
Lord of the Shore, the Islands and the Sea
I shall begin, and end, with you.
   Greece needs good words. Like them or not, the credit will
      be yours.
Determined. Keen to fight, that is our Diomed –
As I should know. When just a boy of 10 I fought
Blowback of Missolonghi, a cannibal, drank blood,
He captured you, he buggered you, you never walked again.
But Diomed lacks experience.
   God has saved us, momentarily.
God loves Achilles.
You took, and you have kept, Achilles' riband she.'

'I was a fool!'

'And now you must appease him, Agamemnon.
Humble words. Hands shaken. Gifts.'

The King – wiping his eyes:

'As usual,
Pylos has said the only things worth hearing.
I was mad to take the she.

I shall pay fitting damages.
Plus her, I offer him
The Corfiot armour that my father wore.'

   Silence.

   The sea.

   Its whispering.

   'To which I add: a set of shields.
Posy, standard, ceremonial.
The last, cut from the hide of a one ton Lesbian bull.'

   Silence.

   The sea.

   'And . . . a chariot!
From my own équipe!
They smoke along the ground . . .
They ride its undulations like a breeze . . .'

   The sea.

   'Plus: six horses – saddled, bridled and caparisoned,
Their grooms and veterinarians . . .

   . . . And six tall shes:
Two good dancers, two good stitchers, two good cooks.
All capable of bearing boys . . .

   'Oh, very well then: twenty loaves of gold,
The same of silver, and the same of iron.'

Masks. Lights.
Behind the lords
Some hundreds from the army have walked up.

Lord Nestor smiles.
Lord Menelaos smiles.

'Plus –
Though it may well reduce your King to destitution:
    A'kimi'kúriex,
My summer palace by the Argive sea,
Its lawns, its terraces, its curtains in whose depths
Larks dive above a field of waving lilies
And fishscale-breakers shatter on blue rocks.
Then, as he draws their silky heights aside,
Standing among huge chests of looted booty,
Long necked, with lowered lids, but candid eyes,
My living daughter, Íphaniss, a diamond
Big as a cheeseball for her belly stud.
His wife to be! minus – I need not say – her otherwise huge
    bride-price.'

'More!'
'More!'
'More!'

Lord Ajax almost has to hold him up.

'The whole of eastern Pel'po'nesia –
An area of outstanding natural beauty –
Its cities, Epi'dávros, Trów'é'zen,
Their fortresses, their harbours and their fleets,
Their taxpayers – glad to accept his modest ways –
All this, the greatest benefaction ever known,
If he agrees to fight. And he admits I am his King.'

Instantly, Nestor:

'An offer God himself could not refuse.
All that remains to say is:
Who shall take it to Achilles?'

Agamemnon: 'You will.'

Starlight.

The starlight on the sea.

The sea.

Its whispering

Mixed with the prayers
Of Ajax and of Nestor as they walk
Along the shore towards Achilles' gate.

'My lords?'

'Your lord.'

'This way.'

They find him, with guitar,
Singing of Gilgamesh.

   'Take my hands. Here they are.'

   You cannot take your eyes away from him.
His own so bright they slow you down.
His voice so low, and yet so clear.
You know that he is dangerous.

   'Patroclus?
Friends in need.
   Still,
Friends.
   That has not changed,
I think.
   Autómedon? Wine.

   '*Dear Lord and Master of the Widespread Sky,
Accept ourselves, accept our prayers.*'

Their cups are taken.

'Father friend?'

King Nestor (for his life):

'You know why we are here.
   We face death.

The mass choose slavery.
Mycenae has admitted he was wrong to wrong yourself.
In recompense he offers you
The greatest benefaction ever known.
Take it, and fight. Otherwise Hector will ignite the ships
Then kill us randomly.
    Can you remember what your Father said
The day when Ajax and myself drove up to ask
If you could come with us to Troy?
That you should stand among the blades where honour grows.
And secondly, to let your anger go.
    Spirit, and strength, and beauty have combined
Such awesome power in you
A vacant Heaven would offer you its throne.
Think of what those who will come after us will say.
    Save us from Hector's god, from Hector, and from Hector's
    force.
I go down on my knees to you, Achilles.'

    '. . . Please . . . No bullying.
Indeed, it is a while since we spoke.'

    A pause.

    'I must admire your courage, father friend,
For treating me as if I was a fool.
I shall deal with Hector as I want to.
You and your fellow countrymen will die
For how your king has treated me.

    'I have spent five years fighting for your King.
My record is: 10 coastal and 10 inland cities
Burnt to the ground. Their males, massacred.
Their cattle, and their women given to him.
Among the rest, Briseis the Beautiful, my riband she.

41

Not that I got her courtesy of him.
She joined my stock in recognition of
My strength, my courage, my superiority.
Courtesy of yourselves, my lords.

I will not fight for him.
He aims to personalise my loss.
Briseis taken from Achilles – standard practice:
Helen from Menelaos – war.

Lord Busy Busy, building his palisade, mounting my she,
One that I might have picked to run my house,
Raising her to the status of a wife.

Do I hate him? Yes, I hate him. Hate him.
And should he be afraid of me? He should.
I want to harm him. I want him to feel pain.
In his body, and between his ears.

I must admit,
Some of the things that you have said are true.
But look what he has done to me! To *me*!
The king on whom his kingliness depends!
I will not fight for him.

Hearing your steps, I thought: at last,
My friends have come to visit me.
They took their time about it, true –
After he took my she none of you came –
Now, though – admittedly they are in trouble,
Serious trouble – they have arrived as friends,
And of their own accord.

But you have not come here as friends.
And you have not come of your own accord.
You came because your king told you to come.
You came because I am his last resort.
And, incidentally, your last resort.

'At least he offers stuff.
All you have offered is advice:

"Keep your temper . . .
Mind your tongue . . .
Think what the world will say . . ."
No mention of your king's treatment of me.
No sign of love for me behind your tears.

I will not fight for him.

I can remember very well indeed
The day you two grand lords came visiting my father's house,
How I ran out to you, and took your hands –
The greatest men that I had ever seen:
Ajax, my fighting cousin, strong, brave, unafraid to die;
Nestor, the King of Sandy Pylos, wisdom's sword.
And then, when all had had enough to eat and drink
And it was sealed that I should come to Troy,
Then my dear father said that lordship knows
Not only how to fight, and when to hold its tongue,
But of the difference between a child enraged
And honour-bound lords.

I will not fight for him.

There is a King to be maintained. You are his lords.
My fighting powers prove my inferiority.
Whatever he, through you, may grant,
I must receive it as a favour, not of right,
Go back to him with downcast looks, a suppliant tone,
Acknowledge my transgressions – I did not
Applaud his sticky fingers on my she's meek flesh.

My mother says I have a choice:
Live as a happy backwoods king for aye;
Or give the world an everlasting murmur of my name,
And die.

Be up tomorrow sharp
To see me sacrifice to Lord Poseidon and set sail.

Oh, yes, his gifts:
"The greatest benefaction ever known."

If he put Heaven in my hand I would not want it.

His offers magnify himself.
   Likewise his child.
I do not want to trash the girl.
She is like me. Bad luck to have poor friends.
Bad luck to have his kingship as your sire.
   My father will select my wife.
Each spring a dozen local kings drive up
And lead their daughters naked round our yard.
Some decent local girl. My father's worth
Is all the wealth we will require.
   You Greeks will not take Troy.
You have disintegrated as a fighting force.
Troy is your cemetery. Blame your King.
The man who you say has done all he can.
The man who has admitted he was wrong.
But he has not done all he can.
And he has not admitted he was wrong.
Or not to me.
   I want him here, your King.
His arms straight down his sides, his shoulders back,
Announcing loud and clear that he was wrong to take my she.
Apologising for that wrong, to me, the son of Péleus.
Before my followers, with you, Pylos and Salamis,
Crete. Sparta. Tyrins, Argos, Calydon, the Islands, here,
Stood to attention on either side of him.
   That is *my* offer. Take it, or die.

   'Nestor may stay the night.
You, dear cousin Ajax, tell your King what I have said.
Preferably, in front of everyone.'

                              Who said,
As my Achilles lifted his guitar:

   'Lord, I was never so bethumped with words
Since first I called my father Dad.'

44

Notes

15   'A glow came from . . . betokened the divine': cf. Virgil, *Aeneid*, 1, lines 589–90. Trans. Sisson, Manchester.

17   'His head was opened . . . trickling from his mouth': cf Henry Williamson, *The Patriot's Progress*, 1930, p. 117.

21   'cloudy sunshine': Dryden – but I'm not sure where.

44   'Lord, I was never . . . my father Dad': *King John*, Act 2, Scene 1, 466–7.